Give over the Heckler and Everyone Gets Hurt

Black Lawrence Press
www.blacklawrence.com

Executive Editor and Art Director: Colleen Ryor
Managing Editor: Diane Goettel
Book Design: Steven Seighman

Copyright © 2009 Jason Tandon

Black Lawrence Press
8405 Bay Parkway C8
Brooklyn, N.Y. 11214
U.S.A.

Published 2009 by Black Lawrence Press, a division of Dzanc Books

First edition 2009

Printed in the United States

GIVE OVER THE HECKLER AND EVERYONE GETS HURT

Poems by
Jason Tandon

Black Lawrence Press
New York

TABLE OF CONTENTS

PART I

PART II

PART III

For my mother and father

In the palm of one hand
Now the rain falls
From the other the grass grows
What can I tell you

Vasko Popa

PART I

South San Ysidro

The rain fell heavy today.

Monsoon snails bloom themselves
of this desert earth
which gleans thick, sloppy kisses
from silver-slick bellies.
Fatty floes
tucked in from heel to toe,

but there is no hiding
from the clump-quakes of soles.

Their deaths
split-sounds.
Pedestrian murders.

The snails persist.
Rise up through mesa red
while the water runs:
mud pebbles clay trash
churning.

Main street, its dirt
daubed with raw innards
and shell shards,
steams in the sun—

awash with the taste of rain
insatiably swallowed.

League Night

Play is suspended
while old Noonie strings his rotten tooth to a gutter ball.
Bleeding to the foot-fault line, he picks up his spare.

I'm nursing a beer when from behind me
I hear the voice of my nemesis:
Give up, Heckler, he says, with an air of onions and bourbon.
A six-shooter plugs my ear.
We end this outside.

I admit I've told jokes.
His lady (dumb as rocks), his car (a shit heap).

It's balmy for February.
A mist rolls in off the bay.
My nemesis calls a duel, though he knows I'm gunless.
A circle of smokers murmurs to see
something other than an out-of-stater
nabbed in the speed trap.

Nemesis turns and counts.
I look up at the marquee,
its low-wattage mustering KARAOKE and GREAT TALENT.

His seventh pace parts the circle.
On the back of his satin team shirt
Boogity Boogity in a purple arc.

Easter Special

In honor of Christ's resurrection
Mister Donut tops a traditional glazed
with yellow frosting and jellybeans.
A man in shimmering pinstripes orders a dozen.

The girl behind the counter plucks a tissue square
and bends over. Her full black moon rises.
Murmuring through his basement keyhole,
he rocks on the balls of his glinting wing tips.

Her cell phone rings *La Cucaracha*.
She answers, and holds an emerald talon
to us all. The guy last in line walks out,
kind marijuana wafting in his wake.

Men at the Lamprey

They march in plantations,
paddies of golden mansion lights
under red skies, and bucket themselves
down amber-walled cisterns.

Clouds hoist grouses
they long to touch, trucks,
bare buttocks. Smother dead voices
they crane to hear.

They give chase into the trees,
guns and hounds in hock.
Taste tender fat and tire tracks
with their tongues in moss.

Falling from their stools
they snuff out flames in their eyes.
Sweep the sockets for a quarter
to play one last game of pinball.

Lambs Grove, Iowa

See it from the highway vista,
Uncle Al's Adult Superstore, cement and windowless.
One lone car in at least an acre of parking.

Next gas station,
read what's etched in a bathroom stall,
JESUS IS COMING.
Written below by a different hand,
(Better look busy).

Continue west to visit your friend,
a scarecrow with cancer for a brain.
He will be sitting up well past dark
grasping a .22, waiting on that *dang bobcat*
to skulk down the hill.

Wonder who in God's country this Sunday morning
doesn't have their hands dirty or full.

Dog Days

Watching a sunlit splay of leaves
fuzzy through the blades of the box fan,
I think about driving to the shore,
strolling a small town's clapboard Main Street
and testing the animal balloonist
with a pocket full of singles.
I'll lunch on a light mayo lobster roll,
then nap on a bench by the sea.

But the traffic going in that direction
is murder—construction on Route 3, its accomplice.
They're enough to keep me here,
sweat trickling from my temples,
today's news dissolving in my grasp,

as I listen to the neighbor's kids
play Marco Polo in the cool deep
of their in-ground pool,
my dog on the kitchen tile with a bout of jazz head,
that bob he does with his tongue lolling,
eyes half-closed, digging the mellow rhythm
befitting this day of oppression and heat.

Doing Things the Right Way

She asks if I can make a Dutch oven from scratch.
If I can cook rice without water or a pot.
If I've ever eaten rat, or would
if I'm starving and there's nothing else.

She asks me to ask her these things.
I have the soul of a black woman, she declares.
The snowman at my window laughs his head off.
The crackers in the cupboard have grown stale.

I've been trying to tell her that it isn't her.
It's the dolls on her bed made with human hair.
The manners book by the toilet.

She craves an omelet. The eggs I have are rotten.
I hand her three and sauté onions with a dash of basil,
her oiled tongue basting my ear.

Red

Your mother named you tough,
but you complain—
a bum hip, myopic.

You live to drink.
Notarize backseats
officially.

Post your bills
on telephone poles.
Smoke till cotton-throated.

My love has grown
porcelain cold.

I lie
in baseboard heat.
Nosebleeds.

Think of your planet
blues revolve,
butter blonde waterfall—

on a sidewalk moon,
streetlit sagebrush,

beneath or wherever
you want to stamp
or sip me.

Fire in the Great Hawk Colony

It broke on an August day
among the conifer hills of Moosalamoo,
while you and I sat across the way
unforgiving our faults and pride,
stubbing cigarettes in the lawn.
Only when we heard the sirens
Doppler up a mile of switchbacks
did we see the smoke loop above the dark spruce.
You drove us up the hill
K-turning out of every side road.
You wanted to see a charred child's body,
a parakeet's burnt beak thrust through cage bars,
a doll's head with looseygoosey eye.
All we found was an A-frame colony,
a private pond, a red clay tennis court.
We came from the shadows of branches
and pine cones to green sunshine and a thicket
by a bend in the road, raspberries still bursting.
You hopped from the car and filled your shirt
like they were the last fruit on earth.
We ate. The engine idled.
My tongue squnged in the sour mash.
My teeth tightened, seeds in their gaps.
I ground my molars and looked at you
in the driver's seat, dropping redblack berries
from fist to mouth, squinting up the hill
for a sign of smoldering ash.

Park Bench

Splayed on pine slats,
heels mud-dug
under a sun, white and muted.
Steam rises from sodden green.

A little boy,
puddle jumping, squeals.
His cold, yellow coat
clings to his skin.

Love, like rain:
No one knows where, when
the first drop falls
or the last will hit.

Rumble Strip
for R.M.K.

We're stranded at table sixteen,
where a lady boasts her setting and stone.
The ringless smile ivory with such fear
in their eyes the glass rims quake.

After cake-cutting and more champagne,
you drive us home, raving of rebel hordes
looting mines and burning villages. Of legs,
gun-butted jaws, sliced breasts tossed in the dust.

Strangling the wheel, you run the rumble strip.
This desert plain stirs with bovine herds
groaning for the abattoir. Mars, a drop of blood,
the galaxy, bone powder blown.

Immigrant Story

I've failed to donate bags of old clothes
now moldy and moth-bitten.
My closet smells like my grandfather's apartment
I used to search as a kid, thinking I'd find a gun.

He had fought in the Second World War
and there was a hole behind his ear
where my older brother said
a bullet was still lodged.

On Grandparents' Day in school
we recited the Pledge of Allegiance.
Everyone removed his hat, except my grandfather
who didn't rise or try to mouth the words.

He came over for dinner many nights
with stitches in his face and a black eye,
having been mugged walking home
from his weekly game of skat.

Podunk

A spawn of snow fleas in my mud room.
Landlord suggests Raid
or wait till first thaw.
The mice in the attic did finally freeze.

My neighbor asks why his boy
burns gasoline all night,
dragging kegs and women up to the falls.
Early risers are a dying breed.

He keeps his perennials covered
with plastic tubs. When it rains
the hollow drums of a colonial march,
among other things, keep me up all night.

Lady Day

This Saturday morning is so bright through the curtains
I get out of bed, though we promised each other
to sleep in after too much wine and pizza last night,
and walk out of my ground-level apartment past the drainage field,
its run-off rivering down the sewer, to the small parking lot.
All around me I hear birds. Whistles, trills, a frenetic pitch and toss,
the high-low moans you read about in old, gooey blank verse poetry.
I run back inside to tell you about a single black-breasted one
calling so close in a bare tree, I can see the vibration in its throat.
And you, the one I love, jump up naked and take my dog, too.

Thanks for Nothing

Years ago, at a burger joint
north of Albert Lea, Minnesota,
my friend Bill got up to pay
and I went out to start the car.
We were a hundred yards away
when I asked how much he'd tipped.
Nothing, he said.
Why? She topped our coffees twice.
I thought you paid, he said.
What? I thought—and so on.
From Albert Lea across the border to Sioux Falls
we checked the mirrors and over our shoulders,
my turkey club sitting in my stomach like an anvil,
Bill's grilled cheese sliding up his throat.
We thought about our waitress,
how she smiled and called us "Yous boys."
She would come up short that day,
worse, get chewed out by her boss, worse than that
asked to turn in her name tag.
That meal was the only thing I've ever stolen.
Except for some time later,
back on the east coast in debt and without a job,
I swiped two pocketfuls
of spice jars from a Grand Union.
Crushed red pepper, marjoram and dill weed, indignant
that I should pay so much for flavor.

Channeled

The fly butts against the window
in a rhythm of rain-steady trickle.

For such a small thing
to think, to feel that the only way out
is through.

Butting the last wave from its brain,
black thinned legs slow
from a tread-water kick.

I pinch a brittle wing.
This franticism staves off what it knows.

Going Under

The hypnotist who convinced the pants
off a dozen female patients
was sentenced today.

During the trial, I bet he was blindfolded
and his mouth duct taped, so not one note
of his voice or glance from his smiling eyes
could send the court screaming of a falling sky.

When the judge handed out ninety days,
what did catch the room's eye? The waxed
balustrade? The stenographer's cherry polish
depressing keys of shorthand?

Occasionally ducking, the hypnotist dabbed
his upper lip with cuffed hands,
a starved yardbird pecking grainless dirt.

Work

It is my job for life to clear
a glacier from a deserted city block.
I'm given a garden spade
and an orange suit with reflective tape.

The street stretches beyond my sight
into a blue, cloudless sky, and to my right
one brick building, where Rachel sits
dangling her blistered feet over the roof's edge.

She says she's from the Bible.
Her story rings few bells.
In the end, her death in the desert
taught us only that beauty is skin deep.

I tell her the sun has lost its power to thaw
and of a vague sense that I'm saving lives.
I heave the spade into the ice and feel no muscle strain,
only the chips that fly and tick my face.

The ice re-forms. I chisel faster.
Wiping my forehead, I steal looks at her legs
to break this eternity into instants,
to tell my friends at the bar when they ask.

Hot for Early May

I am not what you would call a woodsman
or a boatswain for that matter.
Once while sailing, I tossed an empty lighter into the sea.
Forgive me, then, if I cannot name the animal
scratching inside my air conditioner.

As I sit and type the sun is streaming yellow-green
through the leaves of a massive oak.
Below my window two dogs bark,
the yard staccatoed with piles of their mess.
My car—O my automobile—sitting there in the driveway,
What will it be this month?

I concentrate on the ivy spreading across the aluminum backside
of the neighbor's garage, its red-tipped leaves nosing themselves in spite of gravity.
The houses packed in as far as my eye can see,
and the rooftops, like a slew of buxom arrowheads, plunging into the sky.

On one back porch a woman drinks from a mug of something hot
and smokes what I presume is a cigarette.
She flicks it away and kicks up her feet,
tents her eyes with a magazine, which she drops suddenly,
looking in my direction, and gives me a wave—
no, not a wave—the American sign for
"Please stop staring. All I want is a little peace."

PART II

Opening Night

Lit up on the only marquee in town:
CURLY FRIES ARE BACK.

Toronado

Drunk and imagining tattoos
you suggest a face on my face,
a Chinese guy's face on my face,
your ass on my face.

We contemplate a shamrock.
We like bootstrong chanteys and boiled potatoes
and think, if we had emerald isle ink
smack dab on our deltoids, we might feel
more connected to our families, possibly Catholic.

Two girls join us at the table
eating hot pizza from their purses.
They suggest a mermaid, and I am slapped
for illustrating the bouncing boob routine.

I feed the jukebox an ashtray's worth of quarters,
punch in birthdays I can remember.
To the bartender I make the international sign for
"Do my songs stand a chance of playing tonight?"

The girls rattle the bathroom door
hurrying the poor sap on the throne.
You are no doubt at the table,
slicking your hair back with nose grease
and pinching the skin below your eyes.

In Loco Parentis

for Stephen Jackson

The vein in your temple
resembles a earthworm wriggling through the soil.
You now drink three glasses of wine with dinner
instead of one.

You missed your baby's first step,
lorded over you like the unread newspaper
on the porch. A headline of revolt
above a bulldozed pile of shoes.

Your car sits stalled in the driveway,
your father's pawn-worthy clubs
cobwebbed in the basement.
Diapers and wipes don't grow on trees.

Rise and fight at the ding of dawn.
Cave the windshield with one swing.
Spit your blood into a tin pail
for the nice homes here on North Street.

Or go back to Birmingham,
your sunshine, courtesy, and warm corn bread.
Daisy Mae best have the lemonade mixed, my friend,
you'll be mighty thirsty when you arrive.

"O Brawling Love"

title from *Romeo and Juliet*, Act I, Scene i

My machine like loon's laughter awakes. She phones
again! Her voice, angel cake, sweet jessamine,
speaks my name, has suffered my indecision.
For days, her thrusts unparried and unseen.
She reminds me I am still in her favor,
coyly, as I *may* have already won
a brand new Lincoln Navigator.
I must hurry, make claim to Prize Validation.
Oh, why does she state her profession?
Her doddering tone preserves pleasantry,
but haranguing gathers on the horizon.
She thrusts once more, would appreciate
her call returned, toll free. This be Regina Wells—
her name for posterity, I retell.

July Fifth

A Middle Eastern guy got jacked in The Flats
despite screaming the three branches of U.S.
government and both state senators.

A car-surfing sixteen-year-old
was sent skidding on her face. She'll live.
Asphalt rash and a bone protruding.

West of Cleveland, a helicopter landed
in a ring of flares and lifted two bodies away:
a woman in her bra and panties, a husband who wasn't hers.

And a young man, dumped, drunk, and jilted
got back at his girlfriend by shooting the only picture
he had of her, the one tattooed on his chest.

I Don't Speak Donkey

Recently I admitted to my friend Bill
that I can't emote.
"No problem," he assured me,
"just write your feelings in this leather-bound diary
I lifted from a gift shop in London."
Will this help you understand me? I asked.
"Yes," he said.
"I will break into your house,
find the diary stashed in your underwear drawer,
and I will pry its tiny lock.
I'll know that you like the way the rain puddles on the roof of your garage,
that you named the finch bobbing in the water, Thampy,
and that you still dream about all of your best friends
from the different stages of your life
living on the same street, barbequing every weekend,
feasting on your tamarind lamb kebobs
while listening to Tired of Bile,
the punk band you played bass for in college,
and watching photo-worthy sunsets
over a block that has no beginning or end,
which is strange
because you always wanted to live alone
on a dead-end trail in the mountains."

Steakjoint

On a bench by the register, we wait for a table.
I stare at the movie poster above our heads
where a Hunk of the Day shields his blond bombshell
and her pyramidal tits from a rain of savage arrows.

Everyone coming in and going out gives us looks.
Yours are longer. Your skin is darker than mine.
I squint at a ballgame on a TV above the bar.
I can't tell who's playing. I can't read the score.

You itch to drive on to Oakland to your white boyfriend,
newly installed telephone, and finish this hassle of moving.
We eat a basket of free peanuts with flatiron gristle
in our noses. You grind shells into the floor, making dust.

In our motel beds, loaded potatoes roil our stomachs.
You saying louder and louder, *Ah the good life,*
the motto on the sign when we entered this state,
draws pounding on the wall from our neighbors next door.

Power

When she told me her life-long secret,
the one that fed her those chalky blue pills
etched with X's, I swore I'd kill the guy.
Funny, she said. Her father had promised the same.

Nights we humped dry. She pushed off, rolled over,
whispered words she hoped I'd say.
But the ones I chose were as soothing
as shellfish in a casino buffet.

When my best friend cracked his Chrysler
into a tree, his bladder bloated
on a quart of vodka and cranberry,
she could not grieve for me enough.

That day I smoked so much dope
she found me under my bed bawling,
lay with me until the sun dumped itself
just outside my window, then let go.

Carol's House of Fortune

New Year's Day

Take off your coat, hand me your palm.
I'm awake and swishing like champagne.
That goose in the trash?
See no reason to make the skunks sweat.
All will be revealed. I only take cash,
and somewhere in this house I have a shotgun.
Think of nothing, no one. I charge a flat rate.
Can't tell your fortune if you think you've got it made.
That smell? Mouse pee. Potent, I know.
Find paw prints in my grains, tails in the dust!
Poison? Don't want them dying in the walls.
Don't want to catch mud fever either.
See double for days, think up was down.
I'll open a window. Breathe deep, relax.
Your eyes are saggy diapers, your face a fallen mountain.
I have a crystal ball somewhere in this house
and a sign on the door that says Open.

Sunday Afternoon in the Park

A man with oil-spill pits rows a dinghy.
His strokes send the pale,
paint-chipped boat
into a large lazy spin.

A woman lies in the hull,
picking her face with pressed-on pearls.
She yawns
like ten years of breathing didn't take.

He wishes a piranha
from last night's late movie
would leap from the pond into her maw
and eat her inside out,

while she begins to doze,
the sun warming her arms and neck,
dreaming he would do the same.

Ars Poetica:
While I Wait for Takeout at the Chinese Restaurant

A white guy I've never seen here works the register.
Two women at a window table poke a Peking duck.
A bald man slurps hot and sour soup from the bowl.

He puts on specs, opens a newspaper,
pulls out scissors, glue, and a scrapbook.
He cuts out a headline and I feel worthless at two thoughts:

he's a sad man with no wife, no kids;
and the time my ex and I screwed in the kitchen,
feeding each other tangerine beef.

I run to my car but my keys are locked inside.
I sit on the curb with a carton of noodles,
split a pair of chopsticks and eat.

Wanting a beer, I walk to the package store
and glance inside the Chinese restaurant, which is empty now
except for the white guy I swear I've never seen.

Cleaning up after the Dog

Pull plastic bag from pocket
and wave it like a flag

or diploma. Make sure many people
congratulate your care
for the community.

Check bag for holes.
Double check.

Inspect stool for odd hues.
Greens, blues, blood.

Evaluate consistency.

You don't want to leave smears
on the sidewalk or grass—no prints.

Getaway must be clean.

Prepare to go in for all of it.
Hold breath.
Grab, clamp, reverse bag, twist, knot, cinch.

Smell hands.

Hold loaded bag high in the air,
assure onlookers that Everything is Okay.

If a cop should cruise by,
his crew cut bristling
in the sun,

hold that bag higher,
so he, too, can salute
your contribution.

The bomb diffused,
the world a little safer, a little cleaner,

will not offend the deep treads
of someone's shoes.

The Actress

Walking home in a heavy drizzle
after a game of darts,
which I won with three consecutive bull's-eyes,
I passed behind the dinner theater
where I heard a woman yell,
I'm dying for love.
She stood outside the stage door
gripping the railing.
I asked for her autograph.
She wrote my name
the date
and in loops and scratches
her name
which I tried to make out the rest of the way
holding it up to the occasional street light,
and when I got inside
my name
the date
and whoever she was
were blue-grey smudges,
like clouds that threaten rain.

Klutz

First date
we take tea
at your place.
Chipped cups.
Krazy-glued saucers.
You tear a curtain down
to watch the snow
pattern evening a blank
in tangerine streetlight.
You play a Bartók dance
on violin, bow
the final note
and knock
the music stand over.
I send us to bed
without dinner or dessert.

Morning, you wipe
cold fog
from the pane,
sweeping off the sill
a wax stub of vanilla
we let burn all night.
A little dipper of moles
leaks down your shoulder,
and when you turn,
nose freckles
like spilled cinnamon
spread to the upper
reaches of your cheeks.
In you, already
my refuge, sweet,
my breakage.

Serious Poem

We are all bumper to bumper, crawling
through the square, where lane lines have faded
and cars permanently double park.
A white Buick jerks to a halt—behind him
a woman, like you might see in pump class
or dropping her kids off at the rink,
honks her horn. Not once, not twice, but three
hearty leans, her face quickly blistering.
What she can't see is the dopey young man
clutching a scratch ticket, zigzagging his way
across the street. And when she does,
her lips mouth words I dare not repeat.

As if They Own the Place

Morning Shift, who never gets
my smokes right, forgot to put pots
in the coffee makers.
I wait to pay for my gasoline.

Enter three Indians in outlet jackets
and rings, chattering Hindi.
They open folders by the Danish
and lividly thumb receipts.

A Tub, browsing the magazines
in plastic, mouths a trip to the zoo—
sea lions bark, somersault,
shimmy, and shit.

He rolls his eyes at the men,
rolls them over to me—the fourth one
in this Kwik-Stop. Exit Tub,
Morning Shift wiping the mess she made.

Behind the University

It was a confederate flag unfurled
three stories down a brick face
on fraternity row
that took my eyes off the road.

The cat I hit didn't die.
It lay there a heaving lump.
A translucent marble dangled
from a nerve, then rolled away.

The cop slipped on gardening gloves,
bagged it by the hind legs.
He refused to take my name.
Its furry white neck wore no collar.

I pictured a little girl
praying before bed tonight.
I was late to teach a class
and my reason felt like an excuse.

Yesterday's Concerns

Out of potatoes, onions,
ketchup, and coffee.

Bar-backing second shift
on a slow night with Charlie,
a rogue soup chef
who didn't trust his taste buds.

The smell of a woman's hair
fading from my pillow.
My dog's bad hips and bleeding gums.

Out of potatoes, onions...

Last Leaves

My friend was served divorce
when the leaves started falling,
a dog and a one-year-old left in lurch.
A trucker hopped up on No-Doz
leaned his semi into my sister's lane
and rolled her to the emergency room.
I threw myself at a twenty-year-old.
You could say I was looking for beauty,
innocence, red skies at night.
At the restaurant, tomato Florentine
dripped from her mouth.
She was taking a class called Germs.
Found strands of hair in her sink,
sometimes felt fatigue. Don't get attached,
she warned, and forked half
my stunned salmon onto her plate.

Burning this last bag, my mind wanders:
morning's news about the refugee hunter
caught trespassing in Meteor,
unloading his rifle into four men,
one woman, and a boy. His sister
calling him a "reasonable person,"
"the nicest." At work, my friend sobs
in the men's room. He stays up nights
teaching the dog to shake paw.
My sister discharged with a limp,
and the twenty-year-old leaving to study in England
with only her three-quarter camel coat
for the snow-defying rain.
She's a vegetarian, hates fried food.
Though warned, I wonder what she'll eat.

First Sign of Spring

By mid-February my knuckles
have dried and swelled until the skin splits
and blood sticks to my papers, clothes,
and people who politely shake hands.

Walking my dog this morning, I see a robin
in a pruned crabapple tree. My dog is too busy
chomping ice by the roadside
to notice something he would usually chase.

The bird's mustard breast, its head
flitting in this glass bottle wind,
stays treed even as I whistle a call
I know is not his and then try, "Hello."

PART III

Joint Operation

The woman next to me hasn't flown
in seventeen years and wonders
if she'll have time to grab her bag
in Fort Worth and check it onto Cedar Falls.
Things have changed, I say.

This reminds her of her son,
who went to college, eloped, divorced,
and now hangs wanted in the post office
for thirty thousand dollars in child support.
She asks again if she's on the right flight.

The man wearing tinted glasses
and a cowboy hat has had a cigarette
bobbing in his mouth since push back.
Those of us who have walked the aisle
to the lavatory wish he would just light up.

For Our Anniversary

Now that the flowers have dried and withered,
I will tell you that they were a re-wrapped
bouquet—severely discounted—
which allowed me to purchase
those two salmon fillets I glazed
with a bottle of maple dressing,
the crab cakes I served with a spoonful
of spicy mustard from the housewarming sampler
your mother had gifted us,
the package of pre-mixed chocolate chunk
cookie dough I baked from scratch,
and from a fundraising ballet troupe,
that banana nut votive candle
which lasted just the one night.

Social Studies

I've never been shit on by a bird. A friend, who's been shit on twice, told me it smells awful though it looks like lumpy white paint, which reminded me of Mary Catherine Gay giving an oral presentation on the Mayans in front of the entire third grade. She got so nervous her lips chuffed over her horsy teeth and she wet herself. From under her white skirt, a streamlet ran down her leg and soaked her ankle sock. Her piddle spread on stage as the blood in her face. The laughter, the loss of control was reason enough for her to cry forever.

The Dead Man in the Piano

The dead man in the piano is my father.
There is no body, only clothed air,
his raincoat, grey slacks tangled in metal wire,
eight eyelet boots dangling over the side.

Children are not allowed in this room.
Thick blue carpet clean of footprints,
standing three-way mirror in the corner,
an elephant's tusk carved and polished.
I swung it toward the wall once,
stopping just shy of my desire.

A woman dressed in sequins sits upon the bench,
her long hair sprinkled with ashes.
In between faces of gaunt music making
she scans to see if anyone is watching.
Her hands arch off the soundless keys.

A clown, of course, is practicing faces in the mirror,
tired of birthday parties and splattering paint.
This is how it goes. The baby grand's back opens and closes,
the hammers strike. The clown wants out of his day job,
and the woman, admiration from the room.

Brisas del Verde

Dog asleep
in the road
doesn't budge

for a van full
of gringos
until

abuelo
with his spade
yells and

chases its three
bent legs into
the copper grass.

*

At The Shack
Esmeralda hacks
whole chickens

with machete,
packs us
tostones

pollo asado,
no *yuca*—
too hard

she says, and offers
a bottle,
Gato Negro.

      *

Near the hut
where we'll sleep
ferns and red

bromeliads
grow under
dwarf palms

in this rain
forest,
the sun

pinks, mosquitoes
swarm despite
woodstove smoke.

      *

Cucaracha
pokes his head
from a crack

in the plaster,
my head-
lamp beam

scares it back,
but it drops
later

clicks across my face—
I awake
like firework.

        *

I lie atop
El Yunque,
The Anvil,

skyfaced
in the road,
blue stars so

close when I drink
from the Dipper
I taste tin.

Today's Concerns

My friend complains of a trick knee
and arthritis in both wrists
to a brass-caged love bird,
a gift from his new girlfriend.

He sits on the roof smoking cigarettes
listening to pop ballads
sung by kids a third his age.
His wife left a year ago,
their son trailing her with a fake license
and a Swiss Army knife.

My wife makes the coffee every morning
before she goes to work
and leaves little notes
scrolled in the handle of my mug.

These days I call him less and less.
I try to stop by once a month
with a carton and a new CD,
someone seventeen
and singing it like it is.

I Had Wanted to Be an Archer

We lost an hour today.
Kids race their bikes up and down the block
screaming at pitches my dog cannot explain.
Across the street, Anne-Marie
is scolded by her mother
to stop doing what she is doing.

I am on the porch plucking dead leaves
from a Wandering Jew I have twice re-potted.
In this latest transplant I tore its roots.
All that remains is one broken stalk
which I splinted with scotch-tape.
Perhaps it was my doctoring,
the dank earth caked beneath my nails,
that I decided to plant my own garden,
preside over a plot on my hands and knees,
make multiple trips to the nursery
where Gary will show me the sleekest hand-spade
and strategies to defend my strawberry republic
against clover and quackgrass.

On the sidewalk below
a walkie-talkie phone reminds Tom
to bring the cream cheese.
A car engine starts, then guns.
A single chirping sparrow lands on a power line
and suddenly, the cacophony of bird song
is all I can hear.

At South Station

Ready to uncork an hour of craning
over my shoulder, cops ordering me back
into traffic, of driving around the block
left under the overpass, left down a one-way,
left onto Atlantic, hoping to regain
my Ten Minute Unloading Only space—
when had you emerged?
While I watched the honey locusts
shake off the rain? The new perfume you'd bought,
how could I smell it on your skin
from so far away? How could I see
the silver polish you'd painted on your nails
while you waited for a delayed train?

Breakfast in My Twenties

I'd brew coffee from a can of TV blend,
pull my radio from the wall as far
as it could go, and tune in blues or strings
with luck, that luminous refrain and echo.
Crawl onto my roof, light a smoke, and sit
for five or ten to watch a violet cannon or
a carpet gray unroll, while Baba prepared
for the lunch rush in his deli below.
Grilled tahini chicken, falafel and kebob,
I'd bury my nose in my clothes—
O smoke that poured from the vent!
My lungs breathed blood, raw, fresh, my teeth gleamed white.
I could've run five miles each day,
but there was too much to do and see at night.

Monster

for a high school buddy killed in Iraq

I stand in the drainage field behind my house,
which mounds into a small hill pinioned
with slender trees dropping weight for winter's regimen.
Their branches, bone-thin wings of angels.
I remember when we used to drink
on our old playground after dark
until the cops chased us away.

Beyond the hill, in the dun-colored stalks
of dead cattails, a heavy thing drags through the leaves.
I yell. It doesn't scare. Is it the black bear
that made the neighbor's kid wet his pants
when he heard these young trunks snap?

I close my eyes. I've heard this sound before.
That wacko—pacing the gated bowels
of New York's Port Authority, newspaper
twined to his feet—muttering about pound cake.
He had made the best, sold thousands from his shop.
Who don't like pound cake? I don't. But he grabbed
a fistful of my shoulder and I was taught always
to be terrified of those stranger than me.

Incident at Duck Pond

Some punk has smeared the notice board
with duck droppings,
obscuring the elementary
school's crayon pleas to keep our park clean.

Running the path as if guilty,
I am stalled by a honking gaggle
of geese. The mothers hiss
to protect the young.

You know me, I'm innocent!
I say, easing by the old folks
who lean from their benches for a glimpse
of the blue pike once spotted in these waters.

Give Me a Moment

for Mary Oliver

I am tired
of hearing the child next door
slapped, the cat kicked,
the ten-year-old kid
who calls me faggot
for riding my bicycle to the store.
I am not giving up,
not growing desperate
like I used to.
The river's caramel water
is strewn with petals
from spring's late blossoms,
a lone mallard
waddles its way
through the rain-soaked grass—
when I was sixteen
a girl I had showered with mix cassettes
performed the splits
on the hood of a car
in front of a crowded party
wearing a skirt
and no underwear.
I scooted onto my roof
with a 40 oz.
Ready to plunge to the pavement
I slipped
between a sip and a sob
and the bottle exploded into foam—
it is amazing
that in only one morning
the two cut peonies
on the dining table
have filled this entire apartment
with sweet perfume.

Baking

A rainy morning
has cooled the heat of the week.
The fans have been shut off,
the airy white noise
we are accustomed to talking over
silenced.
I hear you call from the kitchen
that we have an egg, flour, sugar,
but only one overripe banana—
yet I recall, alive in the crisper,
a handful of strawberries
left from the shortcake
I surprised you with
after your tearful announcement
of a shitty day at work,
and at the bottom of the fruit bowl
a pear
both of us have picked up
and passed on for God knows how long.
I hear you dice and mash
mix and murmur
I don't know...
while I recline reading on the porch
in a banana chair of all chairs,
enjoying perfect cross-ventilation
engineered by a variance of storm windows and screens,
anticipating that smell
I believe even Gustave Flaubert once declared
impossible to describe.

The Dreamer

Sitting on a cinder block
in the abandoned lot on Orchard Hill,
eyes blurring with city light,
you loved smoking from your first drag.
Doctor told you that would pass.

This evening, as you walk by a house
flickering with white lights
and a muffled "Silver Bells" from inside,
you remember your first love
dumping you around this time.
Although you don't recall the color of her eyes
or what she smelled like,
you do remember "I don't love you"
and wish you had just one.

Make no mistake, it will taste awful.
You will get a headache. You will curse
how much they cost these days,
throwing the rest of the pack in the trash.
Tomorrow, your lungs will burn
now that you've taken to stair climbing,
and you will moan,
"Why did you let me do that?"
to your wife
as she brews a pot of green tea.

To Dance with the Greasy Puppeteer

To dance with the greasy puppeteer
who hops on one stilt to fill a scorched bowler with loonies,
who plays an Italian love song from a boom box
and grinds Mr. Sparkles against the body
of a little girl.

He talks of traveling the world with nothing
but a rucksack full of pots and pans,
and of a wife somewhere in Nordic country
who vowed on a matchbook never to return.
He learned voices from French TV
and faces from German cinema, his favorite
a dour turkey lamenting a pinwheel glued to its beak.

This is all hobo nonsense, you think,
and will not separate me from my money.
But now he needs one last volunteer for his grand finale.

Who here is happy today?
the performer screams in repeat.
The dilemma: admit happiness
or risk him spotting you slip away,
playing you the fool for children,
making you dance in front of a crowd.

Exclusus Amator

Who hasn't walked miles in winter
or at least in rain, convinced by drink
of the grand romance to throw a stone
in the dark and profess love?

Today in the park, a father yanked
his daughter's arm from her socket
and left her standing by a fountain
without a penny to toss.

Visiting my mother, I watch a bird
fly into a window, stun itself and die.
When she cleans, she means business.
I've hardly started eating, when I'm finished.

Tonight I make macaroni and cheese,
your favorite fattening, orange kind.
The kitchen light illuminates the circles
under your eyes, your hair's lost shine.
We spoon seconds onto our plates.

Blackout

What exactly do you expect to find
under that dashboard hula dancer's grass skirt?
Shouldn't your two hands be on the wheel?

Where are you driving to this late anyway?
I suppose it's not late, just the deception
of a gained hour. Winter's coming, they say,
and you smelled the frost last night before it came
and bayed at the moon like a junkyard dog.
You've brought your cigarettes, your tallboy
clenched between your knees, now what?
(Yes, Orion stands low in the sky. His belly
flops over his belt, fat on port and pig.
You remember Cassiopeia from school
and Perseus, who took Medusa's head home
in a bag. This is no measure of smarts.)

You've had your smoke, finished your can.
Heard a song on the radio reminding you
of the dance when you kissed a girl in the shadows
to make another girl sick, and now you feel hollow.
Pancakes might fill you up.
A cup of coffee will keep you awake all night
standing in front of the bathroom mirror
memorizing each little failure for the next time
you are face to face with someone
and silent.

You drive over the bridge toward town
and think about the ones being bombed now.
A hospital under siege, sidewalks empty.
Let's return to the stars, because it is getting late.
And cold, and very windy outside. You are driving because
the power is out where you came from. No water, no phone.
Even the radio, with brand new batteries, doesn't work.

Passing dilapidated barns, fields of dried-out tobacco,
you look for the ghost of the boy
who was tagged by a Chevy fender, and his dog
with the ratty frayed tail who died days later
(of loyalty we'll say). You remember another girl,
who hanged herself recently in her tiny one-bedroom.
You two went out to the pub one night for beer
and sandwiches, and she told you about the dream
she dreamt every night, about a big house on a lake
where she's asleep upstairs, and a little boy at the foot
calling her to come down, come down to the water.

For a moment you hope the power never returns.
This night sky will always be as bright.
Your eyes will, after several days, adjust to the dark.
You will smell and hear better than you do now.
And you remember your neighbor John
telling about the coyotes that come from the hilly inland
down to the Great Bay. You'll smell their rank musk,
he told you, long before you see them.
At his words you reach for your cigarettes
in the passenger seat, light one, and after some time
hold it out the window, closing one eye
to blot out a star with its burning tip.

Grace

Beneath a sapling cypress, Buddha floats
in lotus position above a crushed red brick sea.
Each thumb to each index finger draws your eyes
to empty space. American competitors
garden gnome and lawn jockey pose boisterously
with fairy-tale photogenics, but this slab of soapstone
has his eyes closed to you. He smiles
as if perpetually boarding an outbound
while a chainsaw clears hemlocks in the nearby reservoir
and a backhoe breaks rocks for a new foundation.
He does not flinch at the blue-headed horsefly
trying to bite his neck.

ACKNOWLEDGMENTS

Grateful acknowledgment is made to the editors and staff of the following magazines in which some of these poems have previously appeared:

The Alembic: "Serious Poem"
Bayou: "Podunk"
The Bitter Oleander: "Rumble Strip," "Blackout"
Broken Bridge Review: "Brisas del Verde"
Cairn: "Ars Poetica: While I Wait for Takeout at the Chinese Restaurant," "Incident at Duck Pond"
The Café Review: "Behind the University," "Lady Day"
The Cape Rock: "For Our Anniversary"
Coe Review: "Toronado"
Colere: "Immigrant Story"
Columbia Poetry Review: "I Don't Speak Donkey"
Controlled Burn: "As if They Own the Place," "Easter Special"
Del Sol Review: "Breakfast in My Twenties," "Doing Things the Right Way"
Eclipse: "July Fifth"
Epicenter: "Going Under"
Euphony: "Men at the Lamprey"
Folio: "The Dead Man in the Piano"
Good Foot: "In Loco Parentis"
Green Hills Literary Lantern: "Last Leaves"
Harpur Palate: "Opening Night"
Hiram Poetry Review: "Hot for Early May"
The Madison Review: "To Dance with the Greasy Puppeteer"
New South: "Red"
OpiumMagazine.com: "Cleaning up after the Dog"
Out of Line: "First Sign of Spring"

Pavement Saw: "League Night," "Steakjoint"
Permafrost: "I Had Wanted to Be an Archer"
Poet Lore: "Klutz"
Powhatan Review: "Work"
Regarding Arts & Letters: "The Actress," "At South Station,"
"Channeled," "Dog Days," "Lambs Grove, Iowa," "Power,"
"Social Studies," "Thanks for Nothing"
Slake: "Park Bench," "South San Ysidro"
Steam Ticket: "Give Me a Moment"
the strange fruit: "The Dreamer"

"Baking," "Monster," and "Fire in the Great Hawk Colony"
originally appeared in *Red Cedar Review*, Vol. 42, 2007,
published by Michigan State University Press.

"Joint Operation" first appeared online as Poem of the Month
(May 2006) on *Four Corners*.

"Immigrant Story" appeared in the anthology *Poetic Voices
without Borders Vol. 2* published by Gival Press.

Twenty-three of these poems were originally collected as
Jason Tandon, *Rumble Strip* (Buffalo: sunnyoutside, 2007).
Reprinted by permission of the publisher.

The epigraph is excerpted from "After the Game" by Vasko
Popa, *Homage to the Lame Wolf: Selected Poems*, translated with an
introduction by Charles Simic. Copyright 1987 Oberlin College
Press. Reprinted by permission of Oberlin College Press.

I also wish to thank the University of New Hampshire for
their generous support during the writing of these poems.

ABOUT THE AUTHOR

Jason Tandon was born in Hartford, CT. He received his B.A. and M.A. in English from Middlebury College, and his M.F.A. from the University of New Hampshire. He is the author of one other collection of poetry, *Wee Hour Martyrdom* (Sunnyoutside, 2008), and his poems and book reviews have appeared in *Columbia Poetry Review*, *New York Quarterly*, *Notre Dame Review*, *Pleiades*, *Poetry International*, *Quarterly West*, and on *Verse Daily*. He teaches in the writing program at Boston University.